MW01678483

This is Always Enough

This is Always Enough

John Astin

NON-DUALITY PRESS
UNITED KINGDOM

NON-DUALITY PRESS
6 Folkestone Road Salisbury SP2 8JP United Kingdom

www.non-dualitybooks.com

First printing August 2007

For more information visit:
www.integrativearts.com

Cover design and layout: Susan Kurtz

Isbn 10: 0-9553999-5-5
Isbn 13: 978-0-9553999-5-4

Contents

III. This That Never Sleeps

IV. The Search

V. This Vanishing Moment

VI. Out Beyond Ideas

Introduction

The path to God, the path to ultimate reality is, as Krishnamurti said, a "pathless land". In the end, there is no path to the ultimate because there is only the ultimate. Everything is made of That, the source and suchness of all things – every tree, every person, every flower, every atom, every star – all of them made of the same ineffable mystery, the wetness in every wave...

We may imagine that we are on a journey back to God, but how can there be a journey to something that is everywhere and everything? We walk to our temples and mosques, our churches and synagogues, our yoga centers and meditation cushions, to find God, to find Truth, but what is sought is already present, present before the first step is ever taken, and present as that very step. What is sought is here before the first thought ever arises to seek It, and It is here as that very thought. Truth is present, before the mind ever imagines it has been lost. But Truth is also the imagining, God seeking God...

We seek God but there is no escaping God for there is only God, only Spirit dancing as everything that is seen, everything that is touched, everything that is felt. We search for something else that will make us happy, some other experience or moment, but the happiness and freedom we seek is already here as this – *this* experience, *this* state of mind, *this* moment. Every breath, every sensation, the clarity, the confusion, the seeking, and the end of seeking, all of them God, all of them the Truth, all of them, enough.

I.

This Constant Lover

This Constant Lover

Awareness –
her gaze is so constant,
our every move
watched
with such affection,
a ceaseless vigil
without condition
or agenda,
silent,
patient,
unrelenting in her
embrace.

There is endless room in
the heart of this lover,
infinite space for whatever
foolishness we may
toss her way.

But she is also
crafty, this one –
a thief who will steal away
everything we ever cherished,
all our beliefs,
all our ideas,
all our philosophies,
until nothing is left
but her shimmering
wakefulness,
this simple love
for what is.

Ever Since I Can Remember

Ever since I can remember
there has been this love
for what is,
a quiet love of everything
and everyone,
a love that loves, not because
some higher authority said
it must
but simply because
it cannot help itself,
simply because it cannot
be other than it is.
This Love *is*
the higher authority
that loves what is
simply because it is,
that loves because
it is not possible for it
to do or be
anything else.

The Innkeeper

Everything is
welcomed here.
The innkeeper
refuses no visitors
but beckons
all to enter –
every thought,
every sensation,
everything
that appears
and then disappears –
all are invited
to the dance,
this endless play
of emptiness
loving form,
and wave
loving sea.

Love Without Interruption

Wanting or not wanting,
seeing or not seeing,
grasping or not grasping,
through it all
silence remains
unmoved,
awake,
a love without
interruption.

The Veil

The veil that seemingly
covers your eyes,
the one you think
is keeping you from
seeing the Beloved –
look carefully
and you will realize
just how beautiful
the veil really is,
for it is made
of this Love
that is everything.

To see beyond this veil
is to realize
there has never
really been one.

Who Is Living You?

You can feel it,
can't you?
The sense
that this life
is no longer yours,
that it has never
really been yours,
that Something Else
is living you,
something that would use
you for Love?

I Know One Thing

I know one thing:
that through it all
there is this love
for everything,
a love that
while not mine
is what I am,
a love that does not
ask, "May I come in?"
but simply enters unbidden
without question
or reason.
We did not make this love
nor can we resist its ways –
this silence that
welcomes all things,
the perfect lover
of what is.

Little Green Shoots

Like those little
green shoots
you see
exploding out
of concrete
sidewalks,
this wakefulness
just keeps
rising up
to meet
whatever
appears –
a force of
love that
simply
will not be
denied.

The Truth and the Me

When the truth
touches us,
when it brushes up
against all the silliness,
all the division, all the struggle,
all the beliefs
and images we try
so mightily to defend
or become free of –
when the truth brushes up
against the mask,
the clownish personality called "me,"
what is seen is just how much
the truth loves,
just how much grace
has already been given.

This is what we are –
this love that knows
no bounds,
no distinctions,
no differences,
even as these may appear
before its gentle eyes,
eyes that love with a
fierceness the mind
can never fathom.
This is the truth
that loves even what
appears as bondage,
which is why the
truth is so free.

II.

Our Argument with What Is

The Story

Rest here and watch.
See how long it takes for
the story to reappear –
that ancient legend that tells us
this is not enough.

Keep watching.

Can you see it happening?
Nothing is missing,
until the mind comes back
to tell us there is,
no problem
until the storyteller returns
to tell us something is wrong.

Can you see?

The whole thing
is made up –
the destination
and the path
to get there.
Every story,
even the one
that tells you to stop
telling stories,
is a lie, a tale of lack
where none
has ever been.

Alone

This that is awake
is utterly alone,
alone in the uniqueness
of this body and mind,
this stream of Life
with all its particular tendencies
and quirky preferences.
Not in a hundred million lifetimes
will there ever be another
quite like it –
this utterly unique expression
of the mystery.

There is no need
to be other
than this
particular wave,
no reason to escape
the aloneness
and find company
in some other.
For somehow,
in some strange way,
in the absolute embrace
of this expression
that is like no other,
there is the taste
of some sameness,
the taste of the One
who is all uniqueness,
the wetness
in every wave.

To keep insisting that the moment be other than it is, is the ultimate madness, is it not? After all, the moment can only *be what it is and nothing else.*

If there is no effort to make what is, *other than it is, there is peace.*

Acceptance is not something you do. It's what you are.

Ego

What we call ego is not really a thing at all. Ego is not an entity so much as it is a movement, a movement of mind that essentially says, "This should not be here; something more is needed." In other words, ego is the resistance to what is. Seen this way, the battle against ego *is* ego.

Why Wait?

Why wait for the mind
to grow quieter
or the moment
to be other
than it is?
Why wait for
some feeling to arise
or for the storms
of conditioning
to finally be still?

What if none of it
were to ever happen?

What if the mind
just decided it would
stay the way it was,
forever restless
and wanting?
What if fear simply chose
to take up permanent
residence in your heart?

Then what?

Does anything really
need to change
for you to be
what you have always been?
Why wait for anything
to change when this moment
invites you in, that you might
taste your Self as *everything* that is?

Rich Beggars

We are like birds,
who flying through the air
keep asking:

"Where is the sky?"

Like fish,
who swimming
in the watery depths
keep asking,

"Where is the sea?"

Like kings,
who feasting
at the table of Life
keep asking,

"Where is
there food?"

How does the truth feel? Like this... and this... and this...

It is only the wanting mind that wants the wanting to stop.

Rest in the silence of not knowing, this uncertainty that has no argument with life.

This is all there is. There can never be anything else.

Every Argument

Every argument
the mind
can conjure up,
every belief
and feeling
that cries out,
"This could
not be God,"
is met by
the sheer force
of this mystery
that welcomes
everything.

We are forever
drowning
in that Love…

No Say in the Matter

All the while we struggle,
trying to be happy,
the Mystery waits,
here
in the center
of the heart,
enjoying a nice
cup of tea
and warming
Herself
by the fire.

With or without
our consent,
what appears
before us is
choicelessly
loved,
choicelessly
embraced
by the Mystery
of this that
is awake.

We really have
no say in
the matter.

The End

Are you willing to give it all up?
The struggle to understand,
the struggle to know who you are,
the struggle to remember God,
and the struggle not to forget
what has been remembered?
The struggle to control
and the struggle to let go of control,
the struggle to find yourself
and the struggle to lose yourself,
the struggle to be somebody
and the struggle to be nobody,
the struggle to be your self
and the struggle to be
free of your self,
the struggle to wake up
and the struggle to remain awake?

Are you ready to be done
with all of it, to come to the
end of your suffering?

Being does not have a problem with the separate self-sense. Being is *that very same self-sense, the taste of I.*

What is being pointed to here is not "yes" as opposed to "no," not a surrender that is in opposition to resistance. This is the yes that has no opposite, the yes that has room in it for both yes and no, the openness that has space even for the closing.

To resist bondage is to fall prey to the illusion that bondage is other than liberation, to believe there is anything but freedom.

What you truly are has never had an argument with life. You have always been in love with this…

The Laughter of This Knowing

Is this wave
rolling onto shore
more meaningful
than the next,
the cold wind
at my back
more significant
than the distant
sounds of traffic
passing by?

Nothing is
really more or
less significant,
no thought
no experience
or moment
more valuable
or worthy
than the next.
Everything is
drenched in the
laughter of
this knowing,
everything free
to come and go
in the vastness of
this playful Heart.

All Strategies Eventually Fail

All efforts to control or manipulate experience represent the separate self's attempts to sustain itself, to stay alive. The "me" is in a near constant state of negotiation with reality – trying to remain in control, to obtain some insight, to have a particular experience or to keep some state or experience from happening.

But the effort to remain awake, no matter how well intentioned, eventually ends in pain, because no state of mind can ever be sustained indefinitely. All states, all experiences are impermanent; all strategies of control eventually fail.

Thy Will Be Done

What would it be like
to just sit
with no intention,
to give up this idea
that the mind
must be guided
or directed?

What would it be like
to give up the habit
of believing that one
aspect of experience
is more worthy
of attention
than the next?

What would it be like
to simply be
with no desire,
an empty cup
overflowing with
the nectar of
wanting nothing?

The reason it doesn't feel like you are "there" is that you have some notion in your head about what "there" (enlightenment, realization, peace) will look and feel like. Enlightenment is what is looking at that notion – and it's looking at it right now. See?

~

The mystery that is aware of this moment has already accepted it, as it is. We can't create this radical acceptance and we are powerless to make it go away, for the very nature of awareness is to accept, without conditions, what is.

~

How could one experience be truer than another when everything is the Truth dancing?

This Relentless Love

No matter how hard
you may struggle
to stay afloat,
how violently
you may cry out,
"No! This cannot
be God,"
you can feel it,
can't you, this
current that keeps
pulling you under,
this force that
simply will not stop.

No matter how hard
we may struggle
to keep from
hearing it
the song goes on:

"This too, My child,
this too…"

This Bickering

I should see a certain way
I should listen a certain way
I should talk a certain way
I should feel a certain way
I should have a certain understanding
I should not fall prey to these illusions
I should be more mindful
I should not think so much
I should accept this moment
I should act a certain way
I should not act a certain way
I should remember who I am
I should be more present
I should be less attached
I should be more spontaneous
I should not be so self-conscious,
and on, and on, and on, it goes,
this endless bickering
with what is…

The Trick Birthday Candle

Even after seeing through the illusory nature of the separate self, that same sense of being separate will likely as not reappear, like a trick birthday candle that keeps relighting itself, regardless of how many times or how hard we may try to blow it out. But what we fail to realize is that our efforts to blow the candle out are exactly what keeps relighting it. After all, who but the imagined self would ever have a problem with the appearance of anything?

There is this fear that the realization that "all is well" will somehow lead us to not care, to become cold and heartless. But actually, it is the realization of "no problem" that liberates true love, a love that asks for nothing because nothing is needed.

Remembering and forgetting – it is just God opening, then closing Her eyes.

As spiritual seekers we think that wanting is the enemy, but there are *no enemies. What we call wanting is simply the movement of Life seeking to know Itself, to taste Itself, to express Itself, again and again and again…*

The Rain Must Fall

The desire for experiences to last, or end, is but one and the same desire and the root of all suffering, for neither is possible. Experiences cannot last nor can they be other than what they are. The rain that is falling outside my window this morning will no doubt stop. But for now, it must fall.

The whole universe is in meditation. Everything is consciousness, awake to Itself.

Oneness is not a particular experience – Oneness is every *experience. Oneness is not a particular feeling or state – Oneness is* every *feeling and every state.*

We seek the One but there is no escaping the One because nothing is outside of it. After all, if something could be excluded from It, It would cease to be the One, wouldn't it?

"Satsang" means fellowship or association with Truth. Everything is satsang.

The Gateless Gate

Because of the tendency to be identified with the content of consciousness, it can be very liberating to realize that consciousness is and always has been free from (not identified with) that which appears within it. But in actuality, there really isn't awareness with objects appearing in it. There is *only* awareness, only Life appearing as everything. And as this understanding deepens, it is seen that no experience is the truth and every experience is the Truth, for there is only Truth. So, no experience need be resisted.

After all, what need could there be to become free from appearances when the appearances themselves are freedom? When what appears is simply met – not by the "me" but by the awake space in which everything arises – whatever appears is realized to be just another movement of awakeness, another expression of Life. Then, every experience becomes a doorway, even though there really is no doorway, for we are always and already beyond the gateless gate.

This Quiet Knowing

Sometimes
I am like a young child,
bursting with a desire
to show you what's been
found hidden in the heart
of everything,
exploding with this
longing to share the
extraordinariness
of this that is seen.

And then
there is this
stillness
watching,
enjoying the
whole spectacle –
a roar of silence
in the midst of
all the laughing,
this quiet knowing
that what appears
so extraordinary
is really
nothing at all.

The Gift of Life

The self
is not some villain
that needs to be vanquished,
but the gift of life itself,
the mystery of existence
knowing itself
as the taste of you.

III.

This That Never Sleeps

Never and Always

A song, never heard
but always hearing,

a truth never known
but always knowing,

a vision, never seen
but always seeing,

a love never felt,
but always feeling...

Long Before We Ever Tried

To meditate
is to realize
what has always
been meditating,
the vast and empty sky
in which the clouds
of meditating
and not meditating
appear and
then disappear.

To meditate
is to realize this sky
that kissed the clouds
long before
we ever tried
to love what is.

Be careful not to rush past the simple sense of being awake, for everything you ever sought resides there.

There is nothing that needs to be done to make awareness shine. It is already shining. This is your nature, the light you have always been…

This that is awake is empty, empty of any effort to get some-where or obtain some-thing, empty of trying to become someone, empty of struggling to be anywhere other than here. It is empty of all these notions about how we might manufacture a moment of happiness or satisfaction, these desperate attempts to keep "what is" from becoming what it must always become – "what was."

This that is awake and the sense of I – they are like two lovers who can't tell where one ends and the other begins.

This Welcoming

Clarity is here,
welcoming all the ways
mind tries to become clear.

Awakeness is here,
welcoming all the ways
mind imagines
it might wake itself up.

Freedom is here,
welcoming all the ways
mind struggles
to break free.

Stillness is here,
welcoming all the ways
mind tries to become still.

Love is here,
welcoming all the ways
mind seeks to find it.

Lost

Where have I gone?

Self
has disappeared
into itself.

Everything is lost now,
night vanishing
into night.

This dazzling darkness
beholds only its Self
everywhere
and therefore sees nothing,
even as it lights
up the world.

Is It True?

Is it true?
Are you really lost,
caught up in the currents
of the thinking mind?

Or can you feel
the cool splash of water
and wind upon your face
as the river rushes by?

Is it true?
Are you really lost,
stumbling along
in some dark forest
of worry or fear?

Or is something here,
something that knows
just how black the night
really is?

Is it true?
Are you really lost,
wandering the shore
in some hazy fog
of forgetfulness?
Or have you always
been here
drinking in the fresh sea air
and marvelling at the wonder
of the grey night?

What is it that is looking at all this darkness and confusion you believe you are trapped in? Can you sense how this that is looking is smiling, even in the midst of all the tears?

Only the mind seeks confirmation, validation and approval. What is awake is simply awake. It is not dependent on or conditioned by anything or anybody. It requires no validation, no approval. It needs no outside authority to confirm or support it. It is its own confirmation.

Whether the whole world forsakes you or bows down before you, you remain as you are.

The Dark Silence

We keep searching
for the light,
but the luminosity
we long for
is not visible.
It is the Dark One,
the root,
hidden from sight
and yet always seeing.

This That Never Sleeps

It would not
be possible
to point
to a single
moment
of slumber
were it not
for the
constancy
of this
wakefulness.

Everything is Awake

Every experience
is awake.

The sound of the sea,
awake.

The breath moving,
awake.

The roar of the
vast impersonal,
awake.

The sense of being
a person
and separate,
awake.

The call of the gull
and the sand on my toes,
awake.

The deep still silence
and the senseless
mind chatter,
awake.

The Bed of Wakefulness

Body, mind,
let them rest upon the bed
of this wakefulness.

All the questions of the mind,
let them rest upon the bed
of this wakefulness.

All the images of your self
and the ceaseless effort
to make them different,
let them rest upon the bed
of this wakefulness.

The personality
and all its wants
and preferences,
let them all rest upon the bed
of this wakefulness.

The projects
of self-improvement
or self-annihilation,
let them rest upon the bed
of this wakefulness.

Let your whole self rest
until there is only the resting,
wakefulness,
abiding in itself.

The Taste of Everything

These thoughts
and the silence
that holds them,
the pleasure, the pain,
the beauty, and the
seeming ugliness –
everything has
this familiar taste,
the flavor of this
that is tasting,
the feel of this
that is feeling.
But this is not a sameness
one could ever tire of
for it is the sweetest nectar
of all, the simple taste
of everything.

What is it that sees the many images you have of yourself, that is wide awake to this thought that keeps telling you that you're still asleep?

Is it really possible to become unaware of this moment, to cease to be present? Where would you go?

The very "I" who is trying to cultivate or sustain awareness is awareness itself.

It is impossible to lose the only thing there is.

Awake & Dreaming

I am awake
and you are awake.
We are the same –
awake and peering
through these forms
that are themselves
the expression of
this wakefulness.

I am awake
and you are awake,
always becoming
yet always the same,
one thing –
fingers,
keyboard,
words,
thoughts,
and the emptiness
from which
they spring,
one substance –
an awakeness that dreamt
it had fallen asleep
and is now dreaming
that it wants to
wake up.

I Dreamt

I dreamt that I
could find my Self,
only to wake up
laughing one day.

Then I dreamt
that I could help
you find it too,
and now I am
laughing even
harder.

IV.

The Search

The Language of God

We've collected
so many ideas,
haven't we,
so many notions
about spirituality
and enlightenment –
what it is,
why we should seek it,
and what we will get
once we have
found it.

But before *all* those ideas,
before the mind spins
one more story about
what is needed,
and how we're
going to get it,
before all of that,
what is here?

Silence.

Keeping the Self Afloat

Even if it appears quite natural and effortless, it actually takes considerable energy to keep sustaining the illusion of a separate self. It seems effortless and easy only because it has become such a habit. But in fact, great effort must be made to continue to hold this illusion together. Can you feel how weary you've grown of this struggle to keep the "self" afloat when all along you've just wanted to sink back into the vast depths of this ocean of nothingness that you are?

Seeking takes us to the door of God, but to continue to search indefinitely only perpetuates the illusion that there is something other than God.

All the spiritual prescriptions and practices – be non-attached, accept what is, be open to experience, do not cling, be compassionate – these are all descriptions *of awareness itself, descriptions of what you have always been.*

It is only the seeker who seeks to be rid of seeking. "Give me a strategy that will enable me to let go of all my strategies!" But even all the seeking and strategizing is It! In other words, seeking is not a problem. It's just another way life moves.

Strategies

Being present... Staying in the now... Surrendering to God... Accepting what is... Keeping attention focused on some object or relaxing attention from all objects... We employ such strategies in order to realize liberation, but the strategies themselves tend to perpetuate the very feeling of bondage we seek to become free of, reinforcing the idea that something else is needed, that what is, is somehow not enough.

Nobody Can Give You This

No teacher or lover, no knowledge or experience is ever going to give you what you truly want. Never in a million lifetimes will it happen. If you think it will, you are still dreaming. No one is capable of giving you the truth of who you are for there is no-thing that stands apart from That! Truth, Presence, God – what is sought can neither be received nor given, for it is the only thing that exists.

Looking in the Wrong Place

What is it that you want? Peace? Love? Happiness? If you continue to look for these in *experiences* of peace, love and happiness, you will forever be seeking because experiences (like the one you are having right now) *always* end. That is their nature. So, if you keep looking for the Truth in experiences, you will forever be chasing it precisely because your experiences of "it" will just keep disappearing – as they must.

The mind hears this and thinks, "Well then, I must stop seeking. I must know *that* experience." But not seeking, as an experience, will also fade. The question is, to whom do the experiences of either seeking or not seeking appear and then disappear? There is no escaping the truth of this impermanence, is there? But who would ever want to?

In order to search for anything – peace, awareness, God, happiness – there must be a belief that what is being sought is not already present. Find out if that's true…

In the end, all strategies are born of mind. They are rooted in the mistaken belief that some method or technique is needed to make what has always been awake, awake… to make what has always been present, present… to make what has always been whole, whole.

As spiritual seekers, our conditioned tendency is to believe that awakening or liberation involves having a particular experience or feeling a particular way, and then finding some method or technique that will enable the experience to remain. And yet, it never does, does it? This is the truth that sets us free…

Powerless

There is something
you are not capable
of keeping or removing,
something that no amount
of ranting, raving,
pursuing or resisting
could ever cause to
appear or disappear.

There is something you
are powerless to
obtain or lose –
this silent and relentless
knowing of what is.

It seems natural that spiritual paths evolved in such a way so as to make desire out to be the bad guy, the problem that must be overcome. For if it is recognized that grasping or wanting is the cause of so much unnecessary suffering, it makes sense that we would seek to be rid of those things. But, alas, the effort to be rid of grasping is itself, grasping.

~

Any thought that this moment is not "it" is just that, a thought. And that thought is also "it." There is no escape...

~

We seek happiness because that is what we are. The search for happiness is the search for our Selves.

~

The effort to end suffering is the very thing that sustains it.

This is Always Enough

The search, whether for love, acknowledgement, God, or enlightenment, arises out of the sense that something is missing. The search is predicated upon the belief that what is, is not enough, that it is in some way a problem. But is that true? Is it *actually* the case that what is here is insufficient, that what is appearing should, or even could be other than it is?

This that is being experienced, right now - is it possible for it to be other than it is? Or can it *only* be what it is and nothing else? The rain must fall until it ceases to fall. The darkness must be here, until the light returns…

This moment that is being tasted, right now, should it really be other than it is? Is it actually possible to know, beyond any shadow of a doubt, that *this* experience should be other than it is? No doubt, our preference may be for there to be something else, something more than just this. But *should* there be?

And while we can certainly say that the search is fueled by this belief that what is presently appearing is not enough, we could just as well say the opposite, that it is the searching itself that creates the sense of lack we seek to be free of, that it is not our unhappiness and discontent that causes us to seek, but rather our seeking that causes us to be unhappy. Perhaps we are not at peace for the simple reason that we are searching for it.

If everything is God, then where are you going to go to find It?

~

We try to be aware, but awareness is already happening.

~

The paradox is that when we stop struggling, stop trying to be present, presence is realized to be all there is.

~

It's really quite simple. We are either resisting what is, or not.

~

The mystery that has birthed the stars and your beating heart knows how to wake itself up.

V.

This Vanishing Moment

Innocence

I have never
beheld this before,
never breathed
this breath,
or felt the taste
of this moment
upon my lips.

This awakeness that I am
knows that nothing is
ever *really* known,
nothing ever fixed,
for it sees with the
eyes of innocence
that what is born
dies the instant it
takes form.

Identity

Identity cannot
survive without time,
for in this timeless
moment, before
a single thought or
memory appears,
before mind reflects
upon what was
or what might be,
there is no identity,
is there?

Identity needs
the atmosphere
of time to breathe.
But here,
there is no air –
here where
time is just
a dream and
you have
never been.

Always Being, Always Becoming

Everything is in a state of becoming something else. Life is constantly on the move, forever turning itself into something new, something fresh, something it has never been before. But often we resist this movement, struggling to sustain what cannot be sustained and control what cannot be controlled.

We seek safety and security in things we believe are permanent – our identities, our ideologies, our religious beliefs. And yet, the energy of life is never fixed but always changing. For what we call "the moment," and every idea we ever held about it, is already gone, already dissolving into the next in a never-ending cascade of creation and destruction. What appears is at the same time, disappearing, the arising and the passing away, a single movement, without beginning or end. This is the preciousness of life, this amazing constellation of feelings, thoughts, sensations, and the mystery of wakefulness that illumines them all, here and then gone in a flash…

And the extraordinary paradox is that this which is ever changing is, at the same time, changeless. A bird, a tear, a star – all the movement of a single life, one ocean dancing as a thousand different waves and yet always remaining itself.

Living Dharma

Why cling to some idea
or philosophy uttered
thousands of years
(or maybe just a moment) ago?
Why, when there is already
this explosion of life,
would we ever look back?

The real dharma lives here,
breathing as *this* that has
never been seen
or heard before –
this symphony of sounds
and sensations right now –
the rustle of leaves,
a chorus of birds,
the ache in my back,
the rush of color everywhere,
this wondrous mystery of thought,
appearing then disappearing
like everything else…
This is the *living* dharma,
this timeless presence
that welcomes everything
that has come before but
is defined by none of it –
every teaching, every tradition,
the words you are reading now,
all of them, gone,
consumed in the fires
of this living truth…

This Vanishing Moment

What is here –
is never *really* here
for it disappears
the moment
it appears.
Every thought,
every sensation,
leaving nothing
in its wake,
not even itself.
This that is now
is too small
to measure,
and too vast
to contain,
dying the
moment it
is born
and ending
the moment
it begins.

Flashes of Lightning

Wakefulness –
it comes like a thief
in the night,
lifting the veil
of these dying
memories,
revealing the truth
that the past is over,
that there is no need
to keep looking back
to notice what is
already awake now,
no need to return
to what was once known
in order to realize
what is so alive now.

There really is no
sense looking back,
is there?

No sense gazing upon
the previous moment's
insight or realization,
for it is no longer alive
but only a memory –
a flash of lightning,
appearing
then disappearing
in the empty sky.

VI.

Out Beyond Ideas…

Perfect Kindling

You may think
I am speaking about
some idealized state,
but really this is
the end of all ideals.
Toss them all into
the fire of what is –
they make perfect
kindling.

Enlightenment

There's a wonderful story that comes from the Zen tradition. A student wanted to know what enlightenment was. He kept bugging his master to tell him, but the master kept sending him away, telling him, "I'm afraid if you hear what I have to say, you'll be disappointed." But the young student persisted. So, the master finally agreed to answer his question. "You want to know what enlightenment is?" the master said. "Enlightenment is *you*, exactly as you are."

The Truth of This Nothing

The search for enlightenment or God is a journey back to nowhere – nowhere to stand, nowhere to rest, no identity to land in, no perspective to believe in. It's a demolition project in which every identity, every conceptualization, every experience that was believed to be "It," is finally seen for what it is, pure imagination. In the end, nothing is true. Nothing. And after all the stories about what this Nothing is have grown weary of listening to themselves, what remains is still, just Nothing.

The Truth of Nothing takes it *all* away – all the arguments with what is, all the ideas about how it should appear, all the beliefs about which experiences are It and which are not. There is, as Jesus said, no place for the son of man to lay his head for no experience is it or not it, no feeling or thought or perspective could ever contain the uncontainable. Nothing could ever define what is beyond description. Nothing…

The Question is Made of the Answer

"How can I find God?"
"How can I be happy?"

Such questions are
merely thoughts,
silent sounds rising up
like everything else
out of the Mystery.
They are *made* of
the Mystery.

"How can I find Truth?"

The question itself is
made of the answer.

Beyond

The moment
is beyond
anything we
could ever
imagine
or conceive
about it –
beyond good
or bad,
pleasure or
pain,
beyond freedom
or bondage,
clarity or
confusion.

Gate gate paragate
parasamgate
bodhi svaha –

gone, gone,
far beyond
anything
the mind
could ever
conceive.

No Final Solution

The recognition that the seeker is the sought, that what you call "you" is none other than the very source and substance of everything – this is the end of the journey, the end of seeking for anything else.

But this ending is not really an ending at all for there can *be* no final resolution in a life that is forever creating and destroying and re-creating itself moment by timeless moment. The reality is that every apparent solution, every understanding, every flash of insight, disappears no sooner than it appears. There *is* no final understanding, no final knowing. There is simply life, unfolding.

The sounds that are being heard, right now, are they coming from inside or outside? And the listening – is it inside or outside of this that is being heard?

~

Oneness cannot stand outside of itself to know itself, which is why the Truth remains a mystery even unto itself.

~

Does realization require effort or no effort? It's really a false dichotomy, isn't it? For, if you look at life, can you say whether it's making effort or not? It's really both, and neither. Effortless effort…

A Trip to the Mall

Sitting in the mall one afternoon, a woman walked by and in a flash the whole dream of the "self," and the dream world it thinks it is living in, came unraveled.

In that instant and all around me, the enormous force of culture and conditioning that had shaped her and all of us was so clear – that which mesmerizes each one of us into believing we are who we think we are, that leads us to imagine some destination we must travel to, some thing we must obtain, some place or experience where happiness resides. All the mental stories about what is real and important – all of it learned, all of it inherited.

And as I watched all the other dream characters passing through their dream worlds, it was simply stunning how well the mass hypnosis had taken hold: how strong and convincing is this idea that we are separate selves who are going somewhere, achieving some important goal, arriving at some critical destination. Everything is a story in the mind, a tale with no intrinsic meaning or importance – until the mind grants it such status.

And then in the very same instant, it was seen that this too was just another story, another viewpoint – one perspective commenting on another. "Oh," the mind says, "we are all just sleepwalkers, walking around in a dream, imagining it to be real, totally conditioned to believe all of this is true and actually important, hypnotized into believing in the dream and the seeming importance of what happens to us, the characters in it."

In that moment it was also clear that that assessment was simply another idea, one point of view questioning another, both perspectives utterly conditioned, both ultimately untrue. In that viewless view, it was seen that the apparent dream is neither real nor unreal, neither true nor untrue, neither important nor unimportant, but simply beautiful.

Stop

Simply stop –
no more struggles
or arguments,
no more stories
or conclusions.

Just stop
and be quiet.

Stop, and *be.*

Now stop, even
from the stopping,
and behold what has
always been stopped,
this presence that can
never move away
from it Self.

Rain

The rain is
falling now;
grass grows wet
and green,
Life,
drinking
Life...

No reason,
no purpose,
no philosophy
or theology
could ever touch
the simplicity
of this.

This Movement

All of this
is the movement
of one thing,
the movement
of a mystery
the mind
can never fathom
but always is,
the movement
of something
we can never know
but always are…

We don't really know what this is, do we? Before there is any translation of what is appearing, before it is named there is simply the mystery – not knowing what it is, but knowing that it is.

~

We are both the same and different, utterly unique and yet made of the same stuff.

~

Jesus spoke of "the peace that passeth all understanding," the peace that is present whether the mind is at peace or not. You are *that peace, the simple feeling of awake-awareness that welcomes both calmness and agitation, the mystery that embraces both states of mind, but is defined by neither.*

Before the Mind Divides

"Spiritual" is really just a label the mind gives to certain events it is conditioned to believe are more worthy or meaningful than others. But what makes one experience more worthy or spiritual than the next? Isn't the idea that you are not having the most profound experience of God right now simply a story in the mind? Sometimes mind tells us that what we're experiencing is sacred. Sometimes mind tells us that what is happening is not sacred. But before we carve experience up in the mind – before we label it as good, bad, desirable, horrible, spiritual or profane – there is a knowing that what is, is sacred and holy, simply because it is. Before the mind divides, there is only wholeness – only whole-liness.

Ordinary?

We struggle to make
the seemingly ordinary
into something else,
something we imagine
would be more extraordinary.
But this is our fundamental error.

Ordinary, extraordinary –
these are nothing more
than dream categories
appearing to a dream character.

Wake up and realize you
have imagined distinction
where none has ever been.

There Is No God Because There Is Only God

I can't become one with God because there is *only* God. There is no "I" that is apart from God. I can't integrate God or Spirit into my work or relationships because God or Spirit is all that exists. In the end, there *is* no God, because there is only God. Which is why I can't really talk about God anymore…

The awareness that you are has never believed a single thought the mind has produced. Only thought has ever believed thought. "That's true." "That's false," thought believing thought – the wheel of suffering…

~

It is only a story in the mind that makes any of this certain or uncertain, secure or insecure.

~

Thinking is just another sense, like hearing or touching, only more subtle. It is another way Life experiences it Self. "I am free," "I am bound" – these are different sensations, yes, but neither one more true or right than the next.

After all, is the touch of a feather more "true" than the cold feel of steel upon your hand? Are the birdsongs in the yard truer than the howling sound of the leaf blower outside your window?

Before

This is good,
this is bad,
this is pleasant,
this is unpleasant,
this is clear,
this is confusing,
this is meaningful,
this means nothing…

What is here,
before all of that?

Is there really a mind you must become free of? Have you ever seen it? Can you point to anything and say, "There, that is my mind"? What we call "mind" is really nothing more than a bunch of thoughts and memories with no real substance, a mist that hovers over the sea at dawn, and then fades when greeted by the morning sun, the light of your own ever-present wakefulness.

To not-know is to be free, free from the prison of your own ideas.

Awareness is free – free from knowing what will happen next, free from knowing what should happen next, free from knowing what anything really is, free from knowing the reason for anything, free from knowing what freedom is.

No Map, No Territory

Would you be willing to abandon, even for one instant, all teachers and teachings, all injunctions and practices, to simply meet what appears in each moment with no guidance or reference points to tell you what is true, or how you must live? What would it be like to no longer be identified with *any* conceptual framework or spiritual philosophy – not yours, not Buddha's, not Jesus', not anyone's? How would it feel to live with no maps, no mental conclusions, no final destinations, to cease to refer to any notion in the mind about how life is supposed to be?

VI.

The Empty Ground

The Groundless Ground

Can you feel the
ground beneath you –
the *groundless* ground?
All that's here
is solid awake-space,
the freedom of having
nothing to hold onto
and nowhere to land,
the certainty
of knowing nothing
and being no one.

All is safe here
for there is nothing
to defend.

Where is this ground?
It is everywhere
and nowhere.
It is the silence
that asks for nothing,
and the deepest
longing of the heart.
This ground you will
never stand upon
but always are.

Silent Retreat

The nametag
says it all:

"I am
observing
silence."

How true.

This is indeed
what I am –
the observing silence,
and everything
that is
observed.

Meditate With This

Meditate with this that doesn't care
whether mind is running wild like a colt
or resting quietly in its stall.

Meditate with this that doesn't mind
if thought keeps weaving its stories
or stops for a moment to listen
to the emptiness it lives inside of.

Meditate with this that welcomes
both restlessness and stillness
and knows that neither is true.

Meditate with this
that could never stray
from what is here
any more than wetness
could leave water.

As mind tries
to keep its constant vigil,
struggles to remain with
breath or sound,
there is something that cannot
leave these things, for it is the
very space that illumines them.

Meditate with this.

Looking Out From Nowhere

For a moment, look –
where are you looking from?

There's nothing there, is there?

Just empty space,
a deep, dark, fathomless void,
so clear, so silent, so vast,
without form, and yet
so vital and alive, so awake.

This is the seat of all knowing,
the very center of everything –
every taste, every sound,
every sight, and sensation.

Yet, there is
nothing there,
here,
in this center
that is no place
and everywhere.

Here where the view
is always clear –
free from any preferences
or fixed positions
even as these may appear
before your empty
and radiant eyes.

Room For Everything

Never arguing
or resisting,
sometimes arguing,
sometimes resisting,
the dream of "me"
and the waking
from it –
there is room here
for everything.

In This

The searching
and the end
of the search
appear in This.
The doubts and
the unshakeable
certainty that I am
appear in This.
The contracting,
the identifying,
the grasping,
and the release from
all of them
appear in This –
This that knows
both remembering
and forgetting.

VII.

Nothing Personal

Who Am I?

When the mind is presented with the question "Who am I?", the tendency is to think that there must be an answer. However, this particular question is not intended to give an answer, but to reveal that there are no answers, to point to the reality that there is nothing that you are, and nothing you are not.

Nothing Personal

Are you awakening
to the truth of who you are,
or is Life simply
seeing Itself? Are you listening to the
wind in the trees,
or is the Mystery simply
hearing Itself as the
rustling of autumn leaves?

Are you falling asleep
again, entering into the trance
of separation and suffering,
or is God simply dreaming
a dream, ever-awake, even
as She appears to slumber?

Could it be that none of it
is actually personal,
not one shred of it ours to claim,
for "we" have made none of it –
neither this that appears
and then disappears
nor these eyes that behold it all?

We are neither the seeing
nor the not seeing,
neither the dreaming
nor the waking from it.
There is no one to blame
for the darkness of this
slumber, nor anyone to take
credit when the light returns.

The Deeper Comfort

The deeper rest
is to realize
there is no one
resting.

The deeper trust
to realize
there is no one
trusting.

The deeper seeing
to realize
there is no one
seeing.

The deeper comfort
to realize
there is no one
to comfort.

Paradox

That which is looking out through your eyes has no gender, no shape or form. What is awake is not black, white or Hispanic, not Christian, Muslim or Buddhist, not Democrat or Republican. Such qualities, however real, can never define the awake presence that is peering out through every pair of eyes. But it is a paradox, for in the case of the life stream that is sitting here, typing these words, Spirit, which has no gender, appears as a man and not a woman. So you see, I am a man but not really a man. The mind cannot fathom this.

Surrender

The fact is
it's not really
possible for you
to surrender,
for "you"
are not.

And yet,
something
keeps calling you,
doesn't it –
calling you
to do just that,
to surrender to
this fact.

Nothing Behind Me

I am awareness.
There is nothing
behind me,
nobody who
is aware,
no person in there
pulling the strings
of this seeing
and beholding,
no wizard behind
the curtain of this
wakefulness that
I AM.

Behind awareness
there is only
more awareness,
nothing else,
just endless space,
an empty clearing
in which the
world appears.

A Heart Without Skin

This that feels
so vulnerable,
and insecure,
the very prison
of sensation we've
struggled so
hard to free
ourselves from,
is none other than
the mystery,
Life itself,
Life that stands
forever naked
and exposed,
unguarded,
without defense,
incapable of ever
closing or
remaining hidden,
a heart
without skin.

No Ghost in the Machine

There is no one to awaken, no ghost in the machine. Only this sparkling awareness remains – this that cannot be seen but is the seer of all. It is so clear. *We* do not awaken; awareness simply notices itself. *We* do not become free; awareness simply sees into its own inherently free nature. *We* do not cease to struggle with life; awareness simply sees that it has never really had an argument with it Self.

It appears as if you are navigating your way through life. But really, life is simply finding its own way, discovering itself, moment by timeless moment.

Presence is really absence, absence of anyone who could ever be present.

From the vantage point of imagined separateness, questions about how to find meaning or purpose, or how to realize God or Awareness and then not lose what has been found, are very understandable. But from the perspective of this that is already awake, such questions, though they may continue to appear, no longer make any sense.

Nothing to Protect

You could try to become more loving, try to purify the mind to think more loving, selfless thoughts. You could try to make your behavior look a certain way, according to some idea written in some scripture or spoken by some teacher. Or, you could find out who you are.

For when this is seen, all those ethical prescriptions regarding how we ought to live our lives will be understood to be *descriptions* of what we actually are in our fundamental nature. They will start to happen of their own accord, simply because it has been seen that there isn't really a self that needs to be protected or defended. There isn't really a separate someone who is lacking anything and therefore in need of getting something else (fame, power, approval, love) in order to make it more complete. When this is seen, there arises an impulse to love that is not driven by any ideals, morals, or religious edicts so much as it is compelled by the force of truth itself, which is love.

For You

I came out
of nothing
that You
might hear
the ocean's
roar
and taste
the beauty
of the
evening
light.

This Human Heart

Everything
I have
belongs
to You.
Everything
I am
is You.
And yet still,
there is
something
in this very
human heart
that keeps
saying:

"Here,
take this
too."

You are poorer than you might imagine, for nothing has ever belonged to you. Body, mind, all thoughts, all desires, every joy and every sorrow – none of them yours. In the end, there is only Life with no one to claim it.

As long as so-called spiritual experiences are occurring to someone ("Wow, I had the most amazing experience the other day..."), we're still in the dream. Awakening reveals the end of the one who has experiences and the recognition that all experiences are That.

The kingdom of heaven is, as Jesus said, right within you, within what you really *are. The whole universe and everything you've ever believed yourself to be – a self, a body, a mind, a personality – all of it appears and disappears in what you are.*

The Sense of Self

It's such an irony, isn't it? The very thing we believe to be the source of all our suffering, the separate self-sense we believe must be transcended, the very illusion we think must be seen through in order to awake – that self *is* the doorway to realization, the sense of "I AM", the mystery of existence, awake to it Self.

I Am The Truth, the Light and the Way

"I am the truth, the light and the way." When Jesus uttered these words some 2,000 years ago, he wasn't speaking about the person who was born, worked as a carpenter, and was eventually nailed to a cross for proclaiming his non-separation from God. He was pointing to the truth of who and what he *really* was, that in him that was never born and never dies. "Before Abraham was, I AM..."

Jesus said that he was "the light of the world." But he also said, "*You* are the light of the world." And when he spoke these words, he was not referring to the dream characters we take ourselves to be, but that mystery of wakefulness in which the thought of you and I appears, the light of consciousness that makes the whole world visible. This is the true I, the I that is life, the I that is the way, the only way, the one Truth besides which nothing exists.

Be still and know that you have always been just this, and nothing else.

I am Life

I am life.
I move freely,
delighting in each
aspect of my Self
that I encounter –
tasting my Self,
drinking my Self,
reveling in my Self,
unfolding as the
fragrance of a hundred
thousand flowers
that bloom
and then die.

I am life,
I move as
everything –
the caged bird,
and the freedom
it craves.

I am both
captive and captor,
the one who liberates,
and the one who
is liberated.
I am everything
but also nothing,
because there is
no-thing that
stands apart
from what I AM.

The Center That Is Nowhere

It's cold and windy outside now.
But here it is warm,
here, where there is no
resistance to the movement
called life, where the argument
with what is has finally been dropped.

It's warm here, here in the center
of everything, where inside and
outside simply make no sense,
where there is just this experience
and the next,
just life, nothing else –
nobody to feel this warmth
but the warmth itself,
nobody to experience this sense
of being home everywhere
and in everything.

Printed in the United States
201407BV00002B/192/A

9 780955 399954